Ground Zero

The War on Terrorism

By Nancy Louis

Boca Raton Public Library, Boca Raton, FL

Visit us at
www.abdopub.com

Published by ABDO Publishing Company, 4940 Viking Drive, Suite 622, Edina, Minnesota 55435. Copyright ©2002 by Abdo Consulting Group, Inc., Pentagon Tower, P.O. Box 36036, Minneapolis, Minnesota 55435 USA. International copyrights reserved in all countries. No part of this book may be reproduced in any form without written permission from the publisher.

Published 2002
Printed in the United States of America
Third printing 2003

Edited by Paul Joseph
Graphic Design: John Hamilton
Cover Design: Mighty Media
Photos: AP/Wide World, FEMA

Library of Congress Cataloging-in-Publication Data

Louis, Nancy, 1952-
 Ground Zero / Nancy Louis.
  p. cm. — (War on terrorism)
 Includes index.
 Summary: Describes the September 11, 2001 terrorist attack on New York City, in which two airplanes were crashed into the World Trade Center, and the rescue and recovery work that occurred afterwards.
 ISBN 1-57765-657-1
 1. September 11 Terrorist Attacks, 2001—Juvenile literature. 2. World Trade Center (New York, N.Y.)—Juvenile literature. 3. Terrorism—New York (State)—New York—Juvenile literature. 4. Disasters—New York (State)—New York—Juvenile literature. 5. Rescue work—New York (State)—New York—Juvenile literature. 6. New York (N.Y.)—History—1951—Juvenile literature. [1. September 11 Terrorist Attacks, 2001. 2. World Trade Center (New York, N.Y.) 3. Terrorism. 4. Disasters. 5. Rescue work. 6. New York (N.Y.)—History—1951-] I. Title. II. Series.

 HV6432.L66 2002
 974.7'1044—dc21
                                                                    2001056541

Table of Contents

Flying Bomb

United Airlines Flight 175 moments before crashing into the South Tower of the World Trade Center.

Target Of Terrorism

THE WORLD TRADE CENTER (WTC) WAS BUILT over a period of 11 years and was destroyed in just 90 minutes. On September 11, 2001, terrorists attacked the United States. At 8:45 a.m., American Airlines Flight 11 crashed into the North Tower of the WTC. Eighteen minutes later, United Airlines Flight 175 slammed into the South Tower. The world watched in horror as both towers burned out of control.

Since the workday was just beginning, it was hard to know how many of the 50,000 people who worked in the WTC were in the buildings. When the first tower collapsed, though, it was clear that very few people were prepared for a disaster of this size. Then the second tower collapsed.

The rubble of the WTC is now called Ground Zero. The term "ground zero" is often defined as the center of rapid, intense, or violent activity or change. The devastation and destruction at the scene of the WTC fits this description. It could take up to a year to clear the massive amount of debris at Ground Zero.

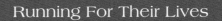

Running For Their Lives

People sprint through debris-strewn streets, fleeing the collapsed World Trade Center towers.

Hours After The Attack

THE MEDIA FOCUSED ON THE WTC AFTER THE first plane crashed into the North Tower. At first, many people believed it was a horrible accident. Then, a second plane crashed into the South Tower. It was now clear that the crashes were not accidents.

Immediately following the WTC attack, U.S. airports and borders were closed to prevent more terrorist attacks. It was the first time in history that all U.S. airports were closed.

All available emergency and public service units in the area were at Ground Zero to help. Police officers helped frightened and injured people exit the buildings. Firefighters rushed up the stairwells to fight the fire, and to rescue people trapped on the upper floors. It was clear that many people would not survive the enormous fire. Ambulances and hospitals were ready to treat what authorities anticipated would be thousands of injured people.

After the attack, New Yorkers were in shock. Confused and scared, people escaped Manhattan on foot. The city shut down. Bridges, tunnels, and subways closed. Many people were trapped in Manhattan until subways reopened later that afternoon.

New York City Mayor Rudolph Giuliani arrived at Ground Zero immediately after the attack. Giuliani organized the city's disaster and financial relief efforts. He mourned the loss of lives, including his friends in the New York Fire and Police Departments. He rallied the spirits of grieving New Yorkers.

President George W. Bush addressed the nation shortly after the attack. He vowed to bring to justice those responsible for

Mass Destruction

A pall of smoke and ash settles over Manhattan after the collapse of the World Trade Center towers.

the terrorist attacks. Leaders from countries around the world sent messages of unity and alliance in the fight against terrorism.

Within 48 hours, officials issued the first arrest warrants. The Federal Bureau of Investigation (FBI) held at least 25 people for questioning. Officials released the names of 19 terrorists who were connected with the hijackings. Officials discovered evidence indicating other attacks were in the planning stages.

Smoldering Ruin

Ground Zero, the site of the World Trade Center destruction, still smolders weeks after the disaster.

Ground Zero

**A**S THE WTC TOWERS FELL, HUGE PIECES OF steel tumbled to the ground, windows blew out, and fireballs engulfed anything in their path. The ground shook violently throughout lower Manhattan. Electricity, water, gas, and telephone services were interrupted.

Thousands of people were buried in the rubble of the collapsed towers. No one knew what to expect as workers immediately began removing debris. They soon discovered that it would be difficult to identify bodies. The explosion and fire had left bodies unrecognizable. The impact scattered or destroyed personal belongings such as jewelry, purses, wallets, and articles of clothing that could have helped workers identify victims.

The air near Ground Zero was full of smoke, chemicals, and dust. Materials used to build the towers, such as asbestos, fiberglass insulation, and concrete clouded the air. Jet fuel fumes were also present. A terrible odor from smoke and burning debris lingered over Ground Zero and the surrounding area. Rescue workers, government officials, and stranded residents wore masks and goggles.

Thick, white ash from the burning rubble coated the area around Ground Zero. People wrote messages of hope, such as "United We Stand" and "God Bless America," in the ash.

Workers found symbols of hope, inspiration, and faith. Many of the huge steel beams lifted from the World Trade Center rubble looked like crosses. The largest cross was saved for possible use in a memorial to be built later. Many volunteers and workers looked to the crosses for strength as they worked endless hours in search of the thousands of missing people still buried under the rubble.

Ash Storm

People choke on the cloud of ash created by the WTC collapse.

Cross of Hope

Father Brian Jordan, second from left, blesses a cross of steel beams found amidst the rubble of the WTC.

WTC Collapse

The South Tower of the World Trader Center tumbles to the ground.

The Towers Collapse

THE WTC TOWERS WERE COMPLETED IN 1973. They were a great example of tube structure architecture. In this type of building, closely spaced steel columns and beams form a tube. An inner core strengthens the tube structures. The 110-story WTC towers were built on six acres (2 ha) of landfill and anchored to solid bedrock 70 feet (21 m) below the ground. This type of building can withstand high winds and settlement.

The planes that crashed into the towers acted like carefully placed bombs. They hit the buildings in high, vulnerable spots. The towers were secured at street level to prevent attacks. The only way to attack the buildings was at a higher level.

The exterior structure of the WTC was made of steel support columns. When the planes hit, they damaged these columns. Then the heat of the fire further weakened the columns. The fire's temperature exceeded 1,000 degrees Fahrenheit (538 degrees Celsius). The intense heat caused the steel columns and beams supporting the building to melt. Soon, the upper floors began to collapse. Within an hour after impact, the towers had completely collapsed to the ground.

Both towers fell almost straight down instead of toppling over. When the planes hit the upper stories of the buildings, the floors above fell onto the impact area. If the planes had crashed lower into the buildings, the structures may have fallen over instead of falling straight down.

The fire from the airplanes' impact was immense. The water sprinkling systems were designed to battle blazes within a few

Cooling The Wreckage

A rainbow forms over the WTC wreckage as firefighters hose the debris.

floors. But in this case, the huge fire engulfed 15 to 20 floors. There was not enough water in the system to put it out.

Many buildings have an emergency exit plan. Emergency evacuation of the WTC was well planned. The plan to orderly evacuate the WTC required approximately two hours. Normally, this would have allowed everyone to escape safely. However, when the buildings collapsed, this was not possible.

A Grim Task

Emergency workers gather at Ground Zero, preparing to search for survivors.

The Aftermath

**A**FTER THE TOWERS COLLAPSED, THE scene at Ground Zero looked like a war zone. Ash and soot caked the area. Papers from the offices in the buildings were scattered like confetti. In the 10-block area surrounding Ground Zero, cars were overturned, debris clogged the streets, and buildings were heavily damaged. Many nearby buildings were in danger of collapsing. When the WTC collapsed, much more than a landmark was destroyed. All of lower Manhattan was affected.

The WTC offices were occupied by many key companies in the financial industry. Thousands of people were able to escape the towers before they fell. Surviving brokers, traders, and technicians relocated to other offices or worked from home.

Many foreign companies also lost employees and businesses. The attack destroyed the U.S. headquarters of five South Korean securities firms and 16 Japanese banks. Some foreign companies gave up U.S. business until they could recover their operations and relocate their offices.

Others were not as fortunate. The NASDAQ, a system that reports on trading in the stock market, lost 19 of its 32 market makers in the WTC. Cantor Fitzgerald, which generates billions of dollars in daily bond trades, lost almost all of its 1,000 employees at the WTC.

Other businesses were not completely destroyed, but they could not operate at full volume. The area around the WTC may have the most telecommunications lines in the world. Twenty percent of the high-speed data lines to the New York Stock Exchange were completely knocked out. The rest were operating sporadically. Engineers feared that the collapse of the buildings caused major permanent damage to the telecommunications network. Once the debris is removed, it will take time to determine the full extent of the damage.

Lehman Brothers used its London and New Jersey offices to coordinate the relocation of its 6,000 employees from the World Financial Center across the street from Ground Zero. Many companies assured their clients that their investments were safe and business would continue as usual. Many financial companies have offices around the world, extensive backup systems, and duplicate records.

Many of the remaining buildings near Ground Zero are unsafe. The first 40 floors of the North Tower contained asbestos insulation. The air in areas of Manhattan may be contaminated for some time. In many buildings, environmental engineers had to make sure the air was safe before people were allowed to enter them again.

Inspecting The Damage

A building inspector peers from a broken window of a pedestrian overpass near the World Trade Center site.

Touring The Disaster

Israeli Prime Minister Ariel Sharon, right, shares a moment with firefighter Frank Piarulli.

The World Comes To Ground Zero

THE NATION'S TOP LEADERS TOURED GROUND Zero a few days after the terrorist attack. About 140 members of Congress inspected the devastation. Senate Minority Leader Trent Lott said he had never seen anything as horrible as Ground Zero. Senate Majority Leader Tom Daschle said that the media cannot convey the true extent of the loss at Ground Zero.

Ehud Olmert, mayor of Jerusalem, Israel, said that he is accustomed to terrorism in his country. He said terrorism is meant to stop people from living their way of life. He urged Americans to carry on as a way of confronting terrorism.

Jacques Chirac, president of France, said that America has the support of the French people. He said that all countries that uphold democracy should fight the threat of terrorism. He thanked the people of New York for their courageous efforts.

Joschka Fischer, foreign minister of Germany, said he was deeply shocked and saddened by the attack. He was impressed by the cooperative efforts of volunteers, emergency workers, and families in New York.

Jean Chretien, prime minister of Canada, said Canadians support their neighbors in the fight to end terrorism and bring to justice the parties responsible for such horrible acts against humanity.

Firefighters from around the world came to New York to help. Thousands of volunteer firefighters from the East Coast came immediately. Within days, there were firefighters from all over the country. Firefighters all the way from Italy also came to help.

On September 14, 2001, President George W. Bush visited Ground Zero. He thanked those working at the site. He shook hands with police officers, firefighters, and volunteers involved in the rescue efforts. After President Bush's speech, rescue workers chanted, "USA, USA!"

President Bush declared a national emergency that called up military reservists. Congress supported the president by setting aside emergency funds and authorizing the use of force against those responsible for the terrorist attacks.

The Environmental Protection Agency (EPA) worked to remove asbestos from the streets and buildings. It also set up monitoring stations near Ground Zero. The EPA concluded that some areas had elevated levels of asbestos. Since only long-term exposure can cause lung disease, the EPA determined that the air near Ground Zero was not dangerous to breathe. However, since the smell was very unpleasant, workers at the site wore respirators and masks.

The President Visits

President Bush puts his arm around firefighter Bob Beckwith while touring the devastation of the WTC site.

A parking lot at Javits Convention Center served as the supply center for Ground Zero. Hundreds of volunteers distributed supplies to workers. The center was stocked with emergency items such as flashlights, batteries, and filter masks.

Special respirators, air filters, rubber boots, and work gloves were in high demand. Coordinators printed daily lists of the supplies they needed most. Supply needs changed as rescue workers reached different levels of debris removal.

Donations poured into the disaster area. They included needed supplies such as eyedrops for stinging eyes, Epsom salts for sore muscles, and Vicks VapoRub for nasal relief from the smoke and ash. People donated more than enough clothing, water, and food. Truckloads of extra donations were stored at Shea Stadium, an hour away from Ground Zero.

What was needed most in the months following the attack was money. Organizations such as the Red Cross distributed money to those in need. Volunteers, supplies, and resources will continue to be needed during the long cleanup process.

Facing page: A "Comfort Bag" filled with toiletries, snacks, and a greeting from second graders from the Groveland Elementary School in Doylestown, Pennsylvania, awaits distribution by the Salvation Army at a hangar at John F. Kennedy Airport in New York, September 21, 2001. The Salvation Army gave packages to those in need after the World Trade Center destruction.

Searching For Victims

Two search-and-rescue workers carefully make their way through the WTC wreckage.

Search And Recovery

RESCUERS USED MANY METHODS TO FIND survivors in the rubble. Rescue dogs searched Ground Zero for survivors. Small robots, shaped like mini-tanks, were used to explore pockets in the rubble. Firefighters attached cameras and listening devices to long poles to search in crevices.

The Federal Emergency Management Agency (FEMA) worked around the clock using high-tech radio frequency sniffers to locate cell phones and pagers of missing persons. Communication companies participated in a Wireless Emergency Response Team to support search-and-rescue efforts at Ground Zero.

Despite these efforts, few people were rescued from the huge pile of rubble. Many of those who did survive were badly burned. Others were severely injured by falling debris. Many survivors also suffered from smoke inhalation.

The task of removing the heavy debris was a slow process. Handcutters broke the twisted steel into manageable pieces. When pockets of space were discovered, there was hope that someone may have survived. But hope diminished quickly.

Fallen Comrades

The flag-draped bodies of victims of the September 11 attack are carried from Ground Zero.

The continuously burning rubble also limited chances of finding survivors. Intense heat and smoke filled many areas. Rescue dogs wore booties to protect their paws from the hot debris. Rescue workers went through many pairs of boots that the heat melted. But volunteers persisted in their search for people who may have survived.

One week after the WTC attack, officials continued to refer to the operation at Ground Zero as a rescue mission. Thousands of volunteers still worked around the clock in hopes of finding survivors. But Mayor Giuliani finally admitted that the likelihood of finding any survivors was small. Many emergency workers took time off after being at Ground Zero virtually nonstop since the attacks. In observance of the Jewish new year, Rosh Hashanah, services were held at Ground Zero for workers and their families who relentlessly carried on their search for survivors.

It eventually became clear that no more survivors would be found. The mission slowly turned from a search-and-rescue effort to a recovery effort. As workers dug deeper into the rubble, they began to discover more bodies. The boxes of trauma supplies, dressings, and medications were soon replaced by small Styrofoam coolers to store human remains.

When workers found a body, the recovery process was paused until it was removed from the rubble. It became a ritual that gave dignity and honor to those who lost their lives in the tragedy. The bodies of firefighters and police officers were draped with American flags as they were removed. Priests were present to bless the bodies and console the weary workers in their grim task.

A memorial service was held at Ground Zero one month after the attack to honor those who died. A moment of silence at the same time the attack took place marked the end of a month-long mourning period.

Since the attack, officials have had a difficult time estimating the number of deaths. At one point, the number of dead and missing was estimated at more than 6,500. This number accounted for some people more than once. It also counted those who survived or were not at the towers during the attack. In November 2001, city officials developed new methods to determine the number of dead and missing. Using these methods, city officials believed the death count to be about 3,000.

Charlie Scibetta holds a photo of his wife Adriane, who died in the World Trade Center attacks, while hugging Adriane's cousin, Christine Laurent, during the WTC memorial service on October 28, 2001.

Mementos

A firefighter hands pieces of the WTC rubble to family members of victims.

A Slow Process

A search-and-recovery crew watches as a crane lifts heavy debris from the WTC rubble pile.

Removing The Rubble

THE COLLAPSE OF THE TOWERS LEFT AN extraordinary amount of debris. The towers collapsed onto the underground mall, creating a hole. The hole was more than an acre (.5 ha) in area and six stories deep. There were more than one million tons (907,200 t) of twisted steel and pulverized building material.

Huge cranes removed the debris piece by piece. Forty-ton (36-t) steel beams were cut into smaller pieces. Thousands of volunteers worked nonstop for the first two weeks. Still, not even one-tenth of the rubble was removed. Four construction companies were hired to manage the cleanup process. The construction crews worked 12-hour shifts along with city firefighters, federal search-and-rescue teams, and 200 specialty dogs.

Structural specialists from the Army Corps of Engineers, experienced in earthquakes and hurricane disasters, were at Ground Zero. They worked with the crane operators to make sure that lifting steel pieces would not cause debris to shift, hurting or trapping other workers.

Trucks loaded with debris rumbled through the streets of lower Manhattan day and night. Their route through Brooklyn to Staten Island took them to a field near a landfill. About 800 people, including FBI agents, Federal Aviation Administration (FAA) officials, city police officers, and firefighters searched for evidence among the tons of steel, concrete, and ash.

One of the biggest challenges for the workers was the six-level basement underneath the rubble. It had a shopping mall, parking garage, and subway station. A retaining wall surrounded the underground structure. It was originally built to keep water from the Hudson River from seeping into the foundation.

Debris from the collapse is holding up the retaining wall. The wall must be kept intact while the debris is removed. Steel cables were drilled through the wall and tied to the bedrock to hold it in place. For safety, the subway train tunnels have been blocked with concrete plugs.

High-tech imaging provided by the National Oceanic and Atmospheric Administration showed where debris and water were. This helped crews know where to dig. High-resolution cameras and laser devices provided information that helped workers effectively remove the rubble.

The Office of Emergency Management assessed the structural damage to the buildings around the WTC complex. All seven WTC buildings either collapsed or partially collapsed as a result of the attack. The buildings include the 22-story Marriott Hotel; 5 World Trade Center, which housed judicial offices and the Bureau of Alcohol, Tobacco, and Firearms; 7 World Trade Center, which held the Secret Service, the U.S. General Accounting Office, and the Securities and Exchange Commission office; and 4 World Trade Center and 6 World Trade Center, where the U.S. Customs House was located. The American Express building in the World Financial Center and the Bankers Trust Building also were damaged. Another 13 buildings sustained moderate damage.

BUILDING STATUS
Not Affected
Needs Cleaning
Damaged But Stable Ready for Occupancy With Repairs/Cleaning
Major Structural Damage Occupancy Not Permitted
Destroyed
In Danger of Collapse

September 19, 2001

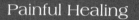

Painful Healing

A flyer describing victim Steven Glick is lit by candles near the Lexington Street Armory in New York.

Moving On

RETURNING TO BUSINESS AS USUAL WAS A slow process in lower Manhattan. Utility crews worked to restore electricity, telephone, gas, and water service to the areas around Ground Zero. About 4,300 businesses were displaced by the disaster. Many relocated to office spaces in other parts of the city or surrounding areas. Some people worked out of their homes. The U.S. Small Business Administration committed millions of dollars in loans to aid homeowners, renters, business owners, and nonprofit organizations affected by the disaster.

It took many months before businesses were operating normally. The city lost over 100,000 jobs as a result of the attacks. But there are some optimistic signs. It will take a lot of work, but some of the buildings that were thought to be structurally destroyed may be restored.

Mandatory carpool restrictions were imposed on private vehicles entering lower Manhattan. Since the area around Ground Zero was destroyed, traffic and parking became more complicated. Carpooling soon became normal procedure to control traffic and pollution.

After the attack, a lot of tourists did not travel to New York City. Mayor Giuliani urged them to return. Tourism picked up again as the Empire State Building and Broadway reopened, along with other well-known areas of interest.

I NEVER
LOVED YOU
MORE...
NEW YORK!

We'll Never Forget

*Flowers and postcards of
the WTC towers decorate a
lamppost near a fire station
in New York.*

Rebuilding

EW YORK DEVELOPER LARRY SILVERSTEIN owned the 99-year lease on the WTC. He said that he intends to reconstruct the buildings in some form. He believes the WTC should be rebuilt to declare victory over terrorism.

Some people think that a modest building or a tribute to the victims would be appropriate. A committee of architects is developing a plan for the recovery of lower Manhattan. Their ideas include a monument, a park, and a memorial. No matter what is decided for Ground Zero, the planning and construction process will take years to complete.

Memorials near Ground Zero, across the country, and around the world honored those who lost their lives on September 11, 2001. The U.S. House and Senate decided to award the Congressional Medal of Valor to firefighters, police officers, and emergency service personnel killed or seriously injured in the line of duty. It will also recognize others involved in the search, rescue, and recovery efforts.

Facts About The World Trade Center

Height: North Tower–1,368 feet (417 m)
South Tower–1,362 feet (415 m)

Compared to other tall buildings:
Eiffel Tower: 986 feet (301 m)
Empire State Building: 1,250 feet (381 m)
Sears Tower: 1,454 feet (443 m)
Petronas Towers: 1,483 feet (452 m)

Stories: 110

Completion Dates: 1972 (North Tower)
1973 (South Tower)

Construction: Tube Structure

Materials: Steel, aluminum, concrete, glass

Environmental concerns: The North Tower was constructed with asbestos insulation up to the 40th floor. In 1971, asbestos, a cancer-causing substance, was banned. The rest of the North Tower and the South Tower were built without asbestos.

Each tower had:
104 passenger elevators
21,800 windows
Almost an acre (.4 ha) of rental space on every floor

Interesting facts:
–The towers swayed three feet (one m) from true center during strong winds.
–From the observation deck of the North Tower, it was possible to see 45 miles (72 km) in every direction.

Timeline

8:45 A.M.   American Airlines Flight 11 crashes into the North Tower of the World Trade Center, setting it on fire.

9:03 A.M.   United Airlines Flight 175 slams into the South Tower of the World Trade Center, setting it on fire as well.

9:30 A.M.   President George W. Bush announces that the nation has suffered a terrorist attack.

9:40 A.M.   The Federal Aviation Administration halts all flight operations at all U.S. airports.

9:43 A.M.   American Airlines Flight 77 crashes into the Pentagon.

10:05 A.M.   The South Tower of the World Trade Center collapses.

10:10 A.M.   A portion of the Pentagon collapses.

10:28 A.M.   The North Tower of the World Trade Center collapses.

10:48 A.M.   Police confirm the crash of United Flight 93 in Pennsylvania.

11:02 A.M.   New York Mayor Rudolph Giuliani asks New Yorkers to stay home and orders everyone south of Canal Street to leave the area.

1:04 P.M.   President Bush promises the U.S. will find and punish the people responsible for the attacks.

1:44 P.M.   Aircraft carriers USS *George Washington* and USS *John F. Kennedy* along with five warships leave Norfolk, Virginia, for the New York coast to further protect the area.

4:00 P.M.   U.S. officials say they believe Osama bin Laden is connected to the attacks.

5:20 P.M.   The 47-story Building 7 of the World Trade Center collapses.

7:45 P.M.   New York officials report that nearly 80 police officers and up to 200 firefighters are believed to have been killed during rescue operations.

8:30 P.M.   President Bush addresses the nation.

Where On The Web?

http://www.people.com
In the search box, type "World Trade Center" to find stories and photos about the attack on America on September 11, 2001.

http://teacher.scholastic.com/newszone/specialreports/under_attack/kids_help.htm
"Kids Make a Difference," a special online issue from Scholastic.

http://www.ci.nyc.ny.us/html/fdny/home.html
The official Fire Department, City of New York (FDNY) web site.

http://www.ci.nyc.ny.us/html/nypd/home.html
Official site of the New York Police Department.

http://www.fema.gov/usr/usr_canines.htm
Canine Rescue: From the Federal Emergency Management Agency (FEMA), this web site explains the canine's role in search-and-rescue efforts. Includes photos and a special kids' page.

Glossary

asbestos

Minerals that separate into long flexible fibers that were used as fireproof insulation. It was used until 1971, when it was discovered that long-term exposure could cause certain types of cancer.

bond trades

Trading of certificates with money value.

brokerage firms

Businesses that trade stocks in the stock market.

fireball

A large ball of fire usually associated with an intense explosion that creates a bright cloud of vapor and dust.

five-alarm fire

The largest and most dangerous call for help that involves fire department emergency assistance from many stations.

ground zero

The point directly above, below, or at which an explosion occurs. After the towers collapsed, the World Trade Center site was referred to as "Ground Zero."

hijack

To take over an airplane by force.

infrastructure

An underlying foundation or basic framework.

memorial

Something that keeps remembrance alive. After the September 11, 2001, World Trade Center disaster, many memorials around the world commemorated those who died.

respirator

Devices worn over the nose and mouth to protect the lungs and regulate breathing.

sniffer

Mechanical device that is programmed to find specific elements, scents, or materials.

terrorism

A systematic use of terror as a means to harm or scare others who do not hold true the same political, religious, or cultural practices and beliefs.

trauma

An injury or wound to living matter caused by an outside element.

Wall Street

Refers to the financial interests that influence the U.S. economy.

Index